TRACTORS

The history, origins, and manufacturers

Contents

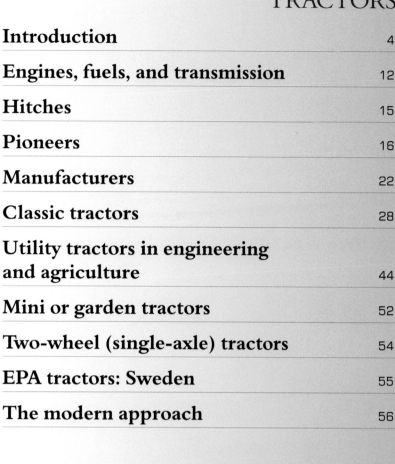

TRACTORS

Published by World Publications Group, Inc.
140 Laurel Street
East Bridgewater, MA 02333
www.wrldpub.com

© Instinctive Product Development 2013

Packaged by Instinctive Product Development for World Publications Group, Inc.

Printed in China

ISBN: 978-1-4643-0232-9

Designed by: BrainWave

Creative Director: Kevin Gardner

Written by: Charlie Morgan

Images courtesy of PA Photos and Wiki Commons

Introduction

Although there has always been much interest in "classic" or vintage cars, vans, trucks, motorcycles, and bicycles, the awareness of old tractors took longer to evolve. However, when it did in the latter part of the 20th century, the interest was phenomenal and worldwide. How many have come to love these old tractors varies from those who flock to events including meets,

■ ABOVE: The Nuffield Universal 4/60 was a 60 hp model introduced in 1961.

reunions, and rallies, to those who remember a balmy summer as children camping in a farmer's field and being allowed to sit on aging relics pretending to drive across the farmland wrapped up in a world of fantasy. But, what these people all have in common, is that they appreciate the character of these special old tractors and recognize the importance and nostalgia of

the hulking ironmongery of a bygone era.

Those that collect, buy, and restore these classic beauties, whether they intend to return them to an as-new condition or simply to ensure that the machinery can be brought back to running order, are certainly helping to preserve an important part of national heritage whichever part of the globe they come from. But what was the purpose of these old tractors in the first place? Today's models are incredibly sophisticated, powerful machines with the latest in hi-tech equipment built for comfort with vibration-insulated cabs and air-conditioning. Tractors now come with satellite navigation, high-capacity hydraulics, and power-shift transmissions designed to meet the increasing demands of intensive modern agriculture. But where did it all start and how did the first steam-powered machines, pioneered at the end of the 19th century, develop into such cutting-edge technology in a high-powered world?

The story of the tractor began in the second half of the 19th century when the first steam engines provided an alternative to muscle power. These steam engines would revolutionize farming methods and would come to replace the traditional method of using animals including horses, mules, oxen, and in some cases,

■ **LEFT: A vintage steam and heavy horse show.**

donkeys. Undoubtedly, some animals working on the land over the preceding centuries would have been treated fairly, but in a world where life was brutal for man, many were not, and a life of toil for animals was often rewarded by literally being worked to death. Life for man was little better and demands for strenuous, repetitive, and dangerous jobs in agriculture continued to ever-increase across North America, Europe, and worldwide. Farming had worked

in this way for thousands of years, despite its inefficiencies in the production of food, and millions across the globe spent their working day on farms with poor conditions in labor-intensive roles.

Due to industrialization and the use of steam power, both in mining and factories, Britain led the way in revolutionizing farming in terms of efficiency and productivity. In 1798, wealthy businessman and farmer, John Wilkinson (1728-1808), known as "Iron Mad Jack,"

■ **BELOW: Loading a late-19th/ early-20th-century threshing machine in a demonstration of steam-powered harvesting.**

changed the course of history when he installed a stationary steam engine on his farm in north Wales to power his threshing machine. From humble beginnings in Cumbria, in the north of England, Wilkinson traveled south where he worked as an apprentice to a Liverpool ironmonger learning how to make cast iron. When his first wife, Ann, died at the age of 23 in 1756, she left him enough money to start his own business, and in 1757 Wilkinson became the owner

■ ABOVE: **A side view of a Birdsell thresher-huller.**
■ BELOW: **John Wilkinson.**

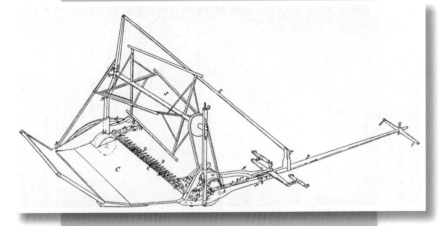

■ ABOVE: A Newcomen steam engine.

■ BELOW: A McCormick reaper, 1845.

of a struggling ironworks at Willey in Shropshire. The Seven Years War of 1756-1763 saw an increase in demand for cannons, and the astute businessman's purchase of the ironworks proved well timed. However, Wilkinson, with an eye on the future, could see the importance of high-quality cast iron parts and began producing components for Newcomen steam engines. A shrewd businessman, Wilkinson became extremely wealthy during the Industrial Revolution in his quest for "truth" – the accuracy of castings. However, he probably did not expect to cover the cost of his engine in just a few short years, and it is likely that Wilkinson installed the engine to encourage other wealthy landowners to invest in steam. By 1799, steam was being used on a farm, based close to a coalmine, thereby reducing fuel costs in East Lothian, Scotland. Records show that steam engines were installed on a number of farms between the turn of the century and the early 1840s, but it seems that many landowners were unconvinced by the usefulness of steam engines; they were still mainly inefficient and expensive. But, a slightly different story was emerging in the United States where farmers were more willing to accept the change in technology, particularly in Pennsylvania and Louisiana where, from 1838, an increase in demand for machinery was evident. Just five years earlier, Cyrus Hall McCormick (1809-1884), had applied for a patent on his "reaper," a laborsaving device, which he had only ever intended to use on his own farm. However, his invention of a grain harvester (still at this time pulled by animals) to replace the handheld cradle scythe proved invaluable and was to become the first in a series of mechanical revolutions in 1800s America which were to change the farming landscape forever. In just 20 years, the McCormick reaper was known throughout the United States and had won numerous prizes and honors including the Grand Medal of Honor at the Paris Exposition in 1855. The reaper soon developed a reputation across the globe and McCormick's company, the McCormick Harvesting Co., joined with others in 1902 to become the International Harvester Co. By the time of the American Civil War (1861-1865), farming devices were developing into mature technology – including the Buffalo Pitts thresher, designed by Hiram A. Pitts, and Jacob Pope's

■ **ABOVE: A Lambert portable engine, 1910.**
■ **BELOW: The entrance to the Farmers Club – 3 Whitehall Court, London.**

■ **RIGHT: Self-propelled "traction" engines moved from farm to farm under their own steam. This 12 hp steam traction engine was used to operate large threshing machines at harvest time. It was made about 1886 by Aultman & Taylor Co., Mansfield, OH.**

Groundhog thresher – and there was a real need for untiring, steady, high-yield power. It was at this time that steam made its debut on the farmlands of North America.

At first, steam engines designed to work on farms were stationary. In Britain, these installations still gained limited acceptance, however, they were revolutionizing the sugar industry in Louisiana, USA, despite their relatively small size, and a breakthrough was imminent when the very first steam engine was mounted on a chassis and four wheels so that it could be towed by horses from farm to farm. This portable engine was to have a huge commercial impact on farming; it made the use of steam more cost-effective by allowing contractors to loan the engine out to groups of farmers who could share costs. In terms of development, the USA and the UK were on a par and technology was taking off on both sides of the Atlantic. Despite these developments, acknowledgement of the first portable steam engine is

9

often given to J. R. & A. Ransome of Ipswich, England, a pioneering engineering company that took up the rights to Edwin Budding's lawn mower in 1832, which was one of the first machines made by the company. James Allen Ransome (1806-1875) became a partner in his grandfather Robert Ransome's firm in 1829, whose Quaker background inspired all his business dealings. His good nature earned him a solid reputation in the upper echelons of agricultural society where he strove to promote advances in technology. He founded an early Farmers Club near Ipswich, which set the model for the London Farmers Club. The pioneering engineer was also one of the first members of the Royal Agricultural Society of England (RASE), which has played a leading role in the development of British agriculture since 1838 through its promotion of science in farming, best practice, and an impartial approach to wide-ranging rural issues. J. R. & A. Ransome took a portable engine to the Royal Show in 1841, where it became a huge novelty with its threshing capabilities. The 1.7 tons of machinery was widely regarded as being able to produce as much power as five horses. The following year, the company followed its

■ **BELOW: Traction engines line up at a vintage steam rally.**

unprecedented success with the world's first self-propelled portable agricultural steam engine, which made its debut at the 1842 Royal Show. This machine, which was to become the predecessor to the steam traction engine, would sell in numbers estimated to be around 8,000 just 10 years after it made its first appearance. The portable steam engine had begun to make its mark on the British market and this attracted interest from across the Atlantic where the potential market was much larger than in the UK. From the early 1850s, traction engines were growing in popularity, and increasing demand saw the advent of the J. I. Case engine in 1869. The company went on to become the largest manufacturer of portable and traction engines in the United States and later worldwide. However, the company went from manufacturing more than 2,250 engines in 1912 to less than 155 by 1922, when tractor power found its way onto the world stage. The US led the way through John Charter's Charter Gasoline Engine Co., based in Illinois in 1889.

Tractors are a truly amazing sight, whether you're watching an old classics race at a rally or admiring the restorations so lovingly pieced back together.

Engines, fuels, and transmission

Following the demise of steam and traction engines (on farms), internal combustion engines, where the combustion of fuel occurs with an oxidizer in a combustion chamber, marked the rise of the modern-day tractor. These engines were powered by the expansion of high temperatures and high-pressure gases, which applied a direct force to components in the engine, including pistons and turbine blades, thereby moving the component over a certain distance. This transformed chemical energy into mechanical energy where, up until the early 1960s, gasoline (which was easier to start from cold) was the fuel of choice, alongside kerosene (paraffin) and ethanol. With its low refining costs, kerosene was offered at less cost than gasoline and made good sense for use in a conventional internal combustion engine.

It was quite usual to employ a small tank of gasoline available for cold starting before switching to the main fuel tank, which would hold the least expensive fuel available in most circumstances. Kerosene, for example, had to be heated by the exhaust gases (produced by the gasoline start-up) in the hot box. Once sufficiently warmed up, the gasoline was switched off and the kerosene tap was opened, allowing the fuel to pass through the hot box where it was vaporized. It was also usual to close the kerosene tap and finish the engine's work on gasoline in order to ensure that there was enough fuel in the carburetor for the tractor's next use. The savings to farmers using kerosene instead of gasoline were quite considerable in many instances. However, gasoline was easier on the engine; costing

■ ABOVE: A 1914 International Mogul 12-25 tractor, a model that had a two-cylinder motor that could run on distillate, kerosene, or gasoline. The Mogul 12-25 was produced from 1913-18 but only 1,599 were made.

■ BELOW: A 1916 International Harvester Mogul 8-16 tractor. The Mogul name was used from 1913 to 1918 and this model, produced from 1915-17, had a single-cylinder engine that could run on gasoline or kerosene.

up to twice as much as kerosene, gasoline was less abrasive and less likely to cause pollution in the lubricating oil. These gasoline/ kerosene-fueled engines required quite high maintenance and it was necessary to change the engine oil following every 50 hours of use (this was increased to 100 hours if only using gasoline). Diesel engines became more popular during the 1960s with 18 hp or above across all tractors, including smaller types for orchards and truck farming and the larger models used on vast fields of bulk crops such as wheat and maize. At the same time, but less popular, liquid petroleum gas (LPG) or propane was also used in tractors, although these required specialized pressurized fuel tanks and filling equipment.

The older farm tractors use manual transmission – also referred to as a manual gearbox – where

■ ABOVE: Produced from 1958-64, the MF65 tractor was available with a choice of gas, diesel, and LPG engines offering a power range of 41-51 hp.

■ BELOW: A manual transmission gear stick.

the driver uses a clutch operated by a foot pedal and a gear stick which transfer the combustion in the engine to the transmission. It is usual for these machines to have several gears (often between three and six) allowing for speeds between 1-25 mph. This enables tractors to be used for steady field work and to travel on the roads between areas. Tractors perform many slow tasks that require them to be controlled, however, traveling on public roads requires a deal of responsibility on the part of the driver, and other road users should be mindful of this and treat the hulking machine slowing their journey with respect. Older models were usually built with unsynchronized transmission, meaning that the driver would need to literally stop the tractor in order to change gear, which caused some problems with various types of farm

■ RIGHT: Driving around using your tractor.

■ BELOW: A 2008 Fendt 312 Vario tractor. This model has a 125 hp common rail turbo diesel motor and, in common with the other Vario models, it has a continuously variable transmission with all of the transmission controls operated through a single joystick.

working. Double clutching and power shifting were the only way around the problem and required the driver to have a degree of skill in terms of speed matching. However, this was dangerous, especially if the tractor was towing a heavy load where loss of control was highly likely. Tractors always had a degree of problems and dangerousness about them and in newer models unsynchronized transmission needed addressing.

Synchronized transmission or continuously variable transmission (CVT) was introduced into tractor design, which allowed for improved gear ratios and enabled the engine speed to match the desired drive speed.

Hitches

A drawbar or hitch system is used in order to transmit the power from the engine to the equipment so that the required work may be carried out for towing. A pulley, or power takeoff system, will be used if the equipment is stationary.

Drawbars were popular for connecting plows to tractors up until the 1950s. A drawbar was simply a steel bar attached to the tractor to which a hitch from the equipment could be joined by a pin (and in some cases a loop and clevis). For early Fordsons, the drawbar was actually part of the rear transmission housing. For convenience, the drawbar could be attached and detached allowing the vehicle to be used for other purposes. Some drawbars were swung so that they could be set either in the center or to one side, and all farm equipment designed to be hitched to the drawbar was given wheels, cultivator, or harrow with a left mechanism in order for the plows, or other device, to be lifted for transportation or for when the tractor needed to turn at the end of a field. However, drawbars were not without danger

and they represented a rollover risk. The short wheelbase on the early Fordsons made these models particularly vulnerable to rollovers. Simple in concept, drawbars were the first design to follow horse-drawn equipment, however, as technology developed, more advanced hitching systems became more readily available. Drawbars – as a useful mechanism – still have their place in attaching equipment to tractors. Front-end loaders, belly mowers, crop cultivators, planters, and pickers were usually applied on fixed mounts designed to complement the tractor they were intended to work alongside. It was, more often than not, impossible to use a fixed mount for one model on a different manufacturer's brand

and tractors were usually stuck with a fixed mount, rendering them unable to do other tasks, due to the inconvenience of removing them and reattaching them on an ongoing basis. It was common practice to mount equipment at the start of a season and leave it there until the harvesting, for example, had finished. It was Harry Ferguson (1884-1960), an engineer and inventor from Ireland, who invented the first three-point hitch in the early part of the 20th century. Using a system of hydraulics, Ferguson designed a three-point hitch, which is raised or lowered by a control lever. This three-point hitch led to the development of the quick hitch, which could be attached to it allowing a single operator to attach farm equipment more quickly and with less danger. Ferguson's three-point hitch was to revolutionize farming, and many of the tractors in use today across the globe use the system or a similar variation. It enables easy attachment and removal of equipment and machinery, and by using a hydraulic lifting ram – which is connected to the upper of three links – the equipment was lifted over obstacles, which previously would have caused rollovers and potentially extremely dangerous and life-threatening situations.

■ LEFT: The three-point linkage and tow hitch implement on a Ferguson TEF-20 diesel tractor.

15

Pioneers

Built as small road locomotives, operated by one man, the first engine-powered farm tractors used steam. Weighing less than 5 tons, these popular machines were replaced by the first gasoline-fueled engine, by John Charter's Charter Gasoline Engine Company, based in Sterling, Illinois in 1889. Known

■ ABOVE: A selection of 2005 John Deere agricultural and turf maintenance machinery. The Deere range covers virtually the entire field of such equipment.

as gasoline traction engines, the machines – of which six were built – were adapted from a Rumley steam traction engine chassis. Another American, John Froelich (1849-1933) from Iowa, was keen to use gasoline power for threshing in 1892, and mounted a Van Duzen gas engine on to a Robinson chassis.

■ ABOVE: The crankcase, toolbox, and operating instructions decal of a fully restored 1929 John Deere Model D tractor. First introduced in 1924, the Model D remained in production in various forms until 1953.

Rigging up his own gearing for propulsion, with exposed gear drive, two forward gears, and one reverse gear, Froelich completed more than 52 days during the harvest of that year using his makeshift machine, and the Froelich engine became widely regarded as the first really successful gasoline "tractor." This pioneering engine was to lead the way for a number of machines, most noticeably the two-cylinder tractor by John Deere. Production of the Froelich single-cylinder gasoline engine, with its 35.3-liter capacity and 16 hp, started in 1892. Meanwhile, William Paterson from California, and his brother James, were also developing an experimental engine for J. I. Case when they filed for a patent in the summer of 1894. This experimental engine did run, but was not considered good enough to be put into production. Although there is not enough evidence to confirm whether this prototype was based

■ ABOVE: The hood of a fully restored 1937 John Deere GP or General Purpose tractor.

■ OPPOSITE: Henry Ford at the controls of one of his first tractors, powered by a 1904 B-type engine, on one of the many farms he owned at that time in the Dearborn area of the US, 1908.

on the first Case engine built in 1892, experts who have studied the patent and the drawings and photographs available, are inclined to think that it was.

Although steam-powered machines managed to hold on to their position for a long time after the advent of portable and self-propelled traction engines, more change was on the way. Traction engines were far too heavy (around 8.5 tons) for the direct plowing of heavy soil – especially soil types found in Britain – and a new, lighter machine, which was gasoline powered, was developed as an agricultural vehicle by Daniel Albone (1860-1906). His tractor design was completed in 1901 and he filed for a patent in February 1902 and, in December that year, formed Ivel Agricultural Motors Limited. The term "tractor"

was little used at this point and Albone called his machine the Ivel Agricultural Motor. Taken from the Latin word trahere, meaning "to pull," the word tractor was first used in 1901, although didn't enjoy common usage until much later. Backed by his directors, including Lord Willoughby, John Hewitt, Charles Jarrott, and Selwyn Edge, Albone's "tractor" won silver medal at the Royal Agricultural Show in 1903 and 1904.

Lightweight, powerful, and compact, the Ivel Agricultural Motor had one front wheel with a solid rubber tire and two large rear wheels (much like a modern tractor today). With its one forward and one reverse gear, the tractor used water-cooling by evaporation. With a 1903 sale price of $480, the Ivel Agricultural Motor could, cleverly, also be used as a stationary vehicle

by the left-hand-side pulley wheel, which allowed it to drive a wide range of agricultural machinery. Of the 500 machines built, many were exported all over the world. With original engines supplied by Coventry company, Payne & Co., and later (1906) by French company Aster, the machine became more powerful – but heavier – and failed to keep up with its main competitors. After a 10-year decline, the company finally went into liquidation in 1920 when United Motor Industries Limited bought its assets.

Henry Ford (1863-1947), an American industrialist and founder of the Ford Motor Company, was a forerunner of mass production. His foresight and proper working conditions – including comparatively high wages – for his employees saw Ford become one of the wealthiest and well-known people in the world. He produced his first experimental gasoline-powered tractor in 1907 with his chief engineer Joseph Galamb (1881-1955). Referred to originally as an "automobile plow," Fordsons were mass-produced as general-purpose tractors between 1917 and 1920 when the brand was subsequently merged with the Ford Motor Company.

Fordson began with the Model F – completed in 1916 – which was to be the first lightweight, mass-produced, affordable tractor in the world. It enabled the average farmer to own a tractor for the first time. The model was first sold in October 1917 for $750 with its 20 hp, four-cylinder, vaporizing oil engine, three-speed spur gear transmission, and worm gear reduction set in the differential. Despite early design and reliability issues, the model quickly established itself across the United States with a market share of more than 70 percent during its early years. Less than a year after its debut, the Fordson had exports in Britain, Canada, and more than 6,000 were in use in the USA. Annual production was

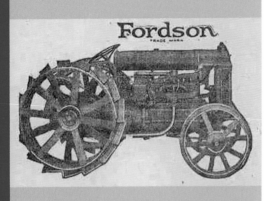

■ ABOVE: A Fordson Model F advertisment.
■ BELOW: The Fordson Model F.

to rocket with sales of more than 36,700 in 1921 and almost 100,000 by 1926. Ford had built 500,000 tractors by 1925, but the Great Depression, which began with the Wall Street Crash in October 1929, saw the market plummet. The company had already ceased its US tractor production (1928) and manufacturing was relocated to Cork in Ireland in 1929. Following this, tractor production was moved to Dagenham in Essex, England, where the Fordson brand was developed on various other models until 1964. Ford continued to manufacture tractors until 1991 when it sold the operation to Fiat.

Alfred Henry McDonald (1883-1963) was another great pioneer of tractors. Born into a baking family in Melbourne, Australia, his father wanted him to join the family firm, but 14-year-old Alf had other ideas; he wanted to be an engineer. He was apprenticed to Henri Galopin

who trained the Australian for four years in electrical and mechanical engineering. Having studied well and gained the respect of his mentor, McDonald registered his company, A. H. McDonald & Co., in 1903, where he worked in a rented room with his younger brother Ernest. It was here that they built their first gas engine and generator set. McDonald was well aware that the age of steam was quickly passing and that the future lay in the development of electricity and the internal combustion engine. He was particularly interested in engines and planned to go into production of machines as quickly as he could. The company moved to larger premises – an iron workshop – in 1904 and called it the Imperial Engine Works, where McDonald's first prototype engine and generator provided the only source of power. The pioneering entrepreneur went into engine production just a year later in 1905. McDonald's A-type engines were 4 hp per cylinder where around 30 models including two, three, and four-cylinder versions were built. By 1907, the company was building D-type engines with 10 hp per cylinder, which was also available in two, three, and four-cylinder models. The following year, McDonald selected the twin cylinder engine for his first tractor in 1908. The first tractor model, powered by the D-type 20 hp engine, was fairly basic although it did have, somewhat surprisingly, dual ignition (coil and magneto) and three forward speeds – there was one in reverse. However, the cooling system was inefficient and bulky and was later modified. In total, 13 D-types were produced up to 1910. From this point, up to 1923, there were numerous tractors of various types and sizes produced by A. H. McDonald.

There were numerous other pioneers of the tractor including Charles Hart and Charles Parr who began their work on gasoline engines in the late 1800s while still mechanical engineering students in Madison, USA. Their hard work paid off when the two engineers opened the first factory in the United States dedicated to the production of gasoline traction engines in 1900 with production of the Hart-Parr No.1, which followed in 1901. George Frick, from Pennsylvania, began building steam engines in 1853 and continued into the 1940s. The Twin City "40" tractor was born when MS&M Co commissioned the Joy-Wilson Company from Minneapolis to design a tractor for them. The company went on to build heavy tractors for other manufacturers such as the Bull Tractor Company and the Case Threshing Machine Company.

M. S. & M. Co. were also pioneering in lightweight tractors when the Twin City model – which was incredibly well engineered

■ **ABOVE:** The radiator name badge of a 1926 Hart-Parr 12-24 tractor.

■ **LEFT:** Manufactured from 1926-29, the 18-36 was at the light end of the range. Hart-Parr was bought by Oliver in 1929 and, for a while, the tractors were sold under the name Oliver Hart-Parr.

■ **BELOW:** Moline tractors.

– went on to become the basis for the Minneapolis-Moline tractor line. During the depressed agricultural economy of the 1920s, M. S. & M. found it hard to survive in a depressed market and began negotiations for a merger with the Moline Implement Company, Illinois and the Minneapolis Threshing Machine Company from Minnesota. In 1929, the three companies merged.

D. M. Hartsough was another influential pioneer of early tractors in the United States. Sadly, there is little information about the man who began conducting his own tractor design experiments around the beginning of the 20th century. It was one of the earliest machines to include a multi-cylinder engine, which helped to power transmission to the rear wheels and give smoother operation. Working alongside R. B. Hartsough and Carlos W. Brewer the company, D. M. Hartsough & Son Co., was building designs that included the Gas Traction and Bull engines.

Hartsough later went on to become President of the Transit Thresher Co. It was Hartsough's early design that was later adapted to become the basis for the famous "Big 4" tractor line, named for their huge four-cylinder engines and overall size. By 1906, Patrick Lyons, of Transit Threshers, was particularly interested in Hartsough's tractor and by the time the company was organized as the Gas Traction Company in 1908, his designs were growing in popularity. The company was bought by Emerson-

Brantingham Implement Company of Illinois who continued to build "Big 4" tractors. These models were heavily promoted in the years before 1920 throughout the United States and Canada at various exhibitions and fairs. But, by the beginning of the new decade, farmers preferred lighter models that were easier to maneuver. It was after 1920 that the "Big 4" were discontinued; however, the part they played in revolutionizing farming across vast prairies would never be forgotten.

Manufacturers

When Froelich proved the success of his threshing machine in 1892, a group of businessmen from Waterloo, Iowa sat up and took notice. The Waterloo Gasoline Traction Engine Company was formed in 1893 to build tractors based on Froelich's design. The original Van Duzen engine was removed from the tractor and used to power the factory. Four new tractors were built with improvements, based on the original design. Steel was used instead of the wood for the main frame, and two machines were sold. However, mechanical problems saw both tractors returned to the manufacturer and in 1895 the company was sold and renamed the Waterloo Gasoline Engine Company. New owner, John W. Miller, turned the company's focus to building gasoline engines. However, the company did put several years into research and development and returned to manufacturing tractors in 1911. The first two years of tractor sales were less than impressive, but in 1913, 20 Waterloo Boy tractors were produced followed a year later by the Model R Waterloo Boy. The tractor was incredibly successful and more than 8,000 were sold between 1914 and 1918 when the line was discontinued.

The Model N – introduced in 1916 – also proved popular with farmers. Both models used kerosene for fuel and the company's Waterloo Boy badge, which was displayed on all tractors, went on to become one of the most famous and instantly recognizable. The Waterloo Boy tractors were clearly ahead of the game in terms of new

■ **ABOVE: A Waterloo Boy engine.**

■ **BELOW: A Waterloo Boy, c1917, pictured at a rally.**

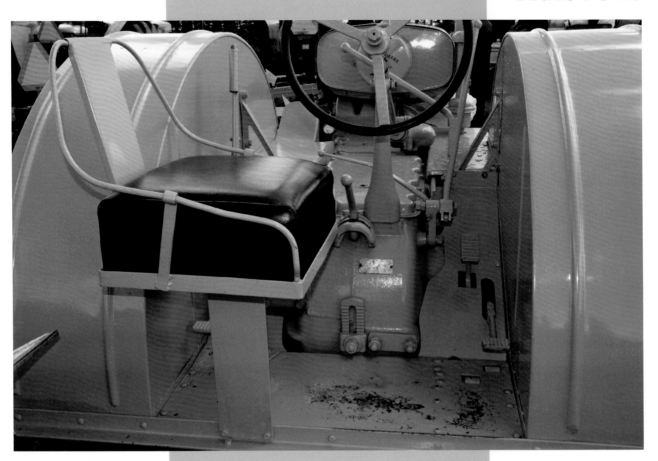

■ ABOVE: The driving position of a fully restored 1937 John Deere D1 industrial tractor. Very few, probably around 100, of these specially colored and outfitted tractors were made. They ran at higher speeds than the farm models, had standard automotive brakes, and sometimes, as with this example, the driver sat in an offset position with modified foot controls.

technology. Popular and reliable, the development of these tractors based on Froelich's original design, came to the notice of manufacturer and farm equipment company Deere & Company from Moline, Illinois.

Looking to break into the tractor market, Deere bought the Waterloo Gasoline Engine Company for more than $3.6 million when field tests of the Waterloo Boy

tractors showed they had the best performance. Deere had been struggling to develop its own line of tractors and initial designs had proved unsuccessful. Following the purchase of the Iowa company, the new tractor manufacturer changed its name to the John Deere Tractor Company; however, tractors continued to sell under the Waterloo Boy name until 1923.

The John Deere Company may have joined tractor manufacturing with failed initial designs and a buyout of successful machines developed by another company, however, it is today, a farming giant with an established reputation the world over. From its unmistakable vintage tractors, first developed in the 1920s, with their distinctive "pop pop" sound and classic

■ TOP: A 2010 John Deere 9670STS without a header attached.

■ ABOVE: A 2009 CLAAS Axion 820. The Axion series is built at the former Renault tractor factory at Le Mans, France, and features engines of 175-230 hp.

green color, to the high-tech models produced today, John Deere is undoubtedly a world leader in tractor manufacturing and has contributed an incredible array of agricultural machines. With unrivaled foresight, an aggressive approach at times, and its determination to become the biggest and the best, John Deere has been (since the advent of its Model D in 1923), and still is, one of the most important and influential manufacturers in the tractor arena. In 2010, the company was listed as 107th in the Fortune 500 and also manufactures combine harvesters, cotton harvesters, sprayers, ATVs, balers, and planters. In addition, John Deere, with its distinctive green machinery, deer logo, and yellow trim, also produces construction and forestry equipment as well as being a supplier of diesel engines and drive-trains used in heavy equipment. The company is also a leading manufacturer of lawn mowers, lawn tractors, and snow-machinery. In order to maintain its world leader status, the company also provides financial services to help support the core business.

Family owned and run G. Marshall (Tractors) Ltd. has been providing machinery to the agricultural industry for more than 30 years. The company's main tractor dealership is with CLAAS, established in 1913 by August Claas in Clarholz, Westphalia. CLAAS began manufacturing straw binders in 1919 following a move to Harsewinkel. By 1930, the company was developing a combine harvester, which was suited to the harvesting conditions in Europe. In 1970, the launch of the CLAAS Dominator 80 saw the most successful series of harvesters introduced on a world stage. In 2003 the product range was expanded to include tractors through the acquisition of a majority stake in Renault Agriculture. By the following year

■ BELOW: **A line-up of 2005 CLAAS tractors.**

the CLAAS tractor was becoming a resounding success in Germany and the 1,000th machine was delivered in Munich. Just five years after acquiring its majority stake in Renault Agriculture, the company was solely owned by CLAAS in 2008, the same year that the versatile tractor, AXOS, with 100 hp, was launched.

Following World War II, Newman Industries Ltd. began operations in Lincolnshire, England, in 1948, building compact, cheap tractors for small farms in order to encourage food production. The company also intended to introduce engineering diversity as Britain began to recover from six years of hardship. The Newman WD2 was a simple design with a C channel chassis and a single-cylinder engine; however, its sophistication came in the form of an adjustable wheel track designed to cope with crop work. In addition, the model had fairly

good ground clearance compared with early models of Ferguson and Fordson. Despite this, the three models built by the company – the WD2, AN3, and AN4/2 – only survived a limited number of years in production.

Established in 1976 as a farm equipment business in Kentucky, Newman Tractors in the USA has fared considerably better than the company of the same name

■ ABOVE: A 1945 Newman three-wheel, an unusual small tractor intended mainly for row-crop use.

in the flatlands of Lincolnshire. The US enterprise has built a solid reputation in the industry for its heavy equipment sales and rental business. Delivering a long tradition of service and loyalty, the company prides itself on its hard work, its much-valued employees, its ingenuity, and strong Christian principles.

Originally founded as the Newcastle Foundry and Machine

■ **ABOVE:** A replica of a 1918 Massey Harris Parrett tractor.

Manufactory, in Newcastle, Ontario by Daniel Massey in 1847, Massey Ferguson Limited was established more than a hundred years later following the merger of Massey Harris and the Ferguson Tractor Company in 1953. Today, the company is a world leader under its brand name, which is used by AGCO. The original firm started out making mechanical threshers by assembling parts from the USA before eventually designing and using its own equipment. Under the direction of Massey's son, Hart, the company moved to Toronto in 1879 where it quickly established itself as a major employer. Shortly after, the company enjoyed considerable expansion and began developing its international sales – Massey would soon become one of Canada's most recognizable brands. The company went from strength to strength for two main reasons: larger US firms were prevented from competing in Canada and a severe labor shortage helped to establish the company's mechanized equipment. Today, the company's machinery, including tractors, combines, and other agricultural equipment, provide top performance, reliability, comfort, and uncompromising quality.

Classic tractors

Actually starting the tractor during the early part of the 20ᵗʰ century was a priority for most farmers. The idea of stopping was less of an issue and brakes were a rarity. Unlike today, where driver safety is a priority, it was paid little attention at the turn of the century, although an exception to the rule was caring and conscientious Quaker, Ransome, who initiated two braking systems on his first model in 1903. One system employed a foot pedal, which disengaged the clutch and applied a brake to the transmission shaft, while the other was operated by a hand brake to the rear wheels. As speeds increased, transmission brakes became essential – although they only operated brakes on the rear wheels. It wasn't until the 1980s that brakes on all four wheels were introduced to some models.

■ BELOW: **A fully restored John Deere, with rear-wheel brakes.**

Waterloo Boy

The Waterloo Boy tractors retained a steel frame structure well into the 1920s and had several claims to fame. First, they introduced manufacturer John Deere to the two-cylinder horizontal engine layout that would remain a successful feature of many of the firm's tractor designs for more than 40 years. Second, the Waterloo Boys – under the Overtime brand name – were exported to a British market where they undoubtedly established further tractor development. The Model N was also the first tractor to undergo testing in Nebraska. The Waterloo Boy established a reputation for reliability and pulling power. Mechanically simple, the tractors, both N and R models, offered better access for servicing than many of their contemporaries, although the R's final drive was based on ring gears – exposed to dust and mud – and wear and tear was inevitable especially in more hostile environments with stony soils. Both models look similar in design with the same layout in engine, transmission, and cooling systems, however, there were design differences made to the Model N including a two-speed transmission and a radiator mounted on the left-hand-side. More than 21,000 of these kerosene-fueled tractors were produced weighing around 5,500 pounds, with horsepower of 12 hp.

■ BELOW: **Mechanisms of a 1918 Waterloo Boy N tractor.**

Full rated power and high quality construction positively guaranteed.

Write for free illustrated catalog.

Waterloo Gasoline Engine Co.,
105 W. 3rd Ave.   Waterloo, Iowa

$750

Pulls Three 14" Plows
Belt Power for 17" Silage
Cutter or 24" Thresher

■ RIGHT: **Advertised in the February 17, 1917 issue of** *Country Gentleman* **magazine.**

29

■ ABOVE: Two John Deere D tractors. In the foreground is a 1928 model and behind it a 1929 model.

John Deere Model D

Incredibly, or perhaps due to its astounding design, the John Deere Model D, a unit construction (built without a frame or chassis), remained in production for 30 years (1923-1953). This was an all-time record for any tractor model constructed with engine and transmission housing bolted together to provide a single rigid unit. The two cylinders were housed horizontally, side by side, facing forward. In its long career, the Model D received various upgrades and improvements. With horsepower of between 15 and 27 hp, more than 160,000 of these steel-wheeled machines were produced.

■ ABOVE & RIGHT: A John Deere Model D tractor, also known as a "Spoker D" due to the spoked flywheel. Beginning in 1926, it was changed to a solid flywheel.

■ **ABOVE:** The Lanz tractors have very low compression and require their fuel to be pre-heated before starting, using a small lamp, seen here in front of the tractors.

Lanz Bulldog

Enjoying a worldwide reputation, including across Europe, Australia, and South America, the Lanz Bulldog was an inexpensive, simple power sourced (single cylinder) machine that was easily maintained and serviced. The tractor was manufactured by Heinrich Lanz AG in Germany from 1921 – where various versions were built – up to 1960. With its two-stroke, hot bulb engine and 12 hp, the engine was eventually improved to 55 hp. The hot bulb engine, while crude, could burn a wide variety of fuels (low grade) and waste oils. This type of engine, developed at the end of the 19th century, was a type of internal combustion engine where fuel is ignited by being brought into contact with a red-hot metal surface inside a bulb.

John Deere purchased Lanz in 1956 and in its long, illustrious career, more than 220,000 Bulldogs were produced. Today, the name Bulldog is still widely used in Germany as a term for tractor.

■ **BELOW:** A 1937 Lanz Bulldog tractor.

■ ABOVE: A McCormick Farmall tractor dating from the 1940s. This example is still in regular use as it has a belt-drive power-takeoff that enables it to run older machinery such as the chaff cutter.

Farmall

Farmall general-purpose tractors first went into production in the 1920s and, for 50 years, were the stalwarts of row-crop work on small- to medium-sized family farms. These robust tractors held a market share for the longevity of their production lives and could perform various tasks, which lessened the need for animals and even laborers. The name Farmall was first used for the models of tractors built, before becoming synonymous with the brand. With nimble maneuverability, Farmall

tractors encompassed narrowly-spaced front wheels (known as a tricycle configuration) and were built with added ground clearance. So useful were these well-designed tractors that they could also greatly reduce farming and agricultural costs providing that they remained reliable and fuel was reasonably priced. Similar to the Fordson in its capabilities, the Farmall was also mass-produced and affordable. Produced by International Harvester, the models were light and designed to be manufactured quickly and easily, however, one oversight might be that the early tractors from Farmall were not

capable of cultivating effectively enough. International Harvester recognized a need for motorized cultivation in the market place.

As a competitor for Fordson, the company had first introduced the Motor Cultivator, a self-propelled cultivator that was a fairly crude machine with a simple motor. International Harvester struggled with their model and soon discontinued the machine after finding that many farmers were content to keep one or two animals for cultivation. The first Farmall tractors were brought to market in Texas, but following their success, the company began mass-production in 1926 in Illinois. In fact, so successful was the company's lightweight machine that it became a firm favorite throughout the United States and prevented Fordson from monopolizing the market as well as outselling the likes of John Deere. The year 1931 saw the advent of the F-30 (commonly known among farmers at the time as the Regular – an unofficial name). The model was upgraded a year later and renamed the F-20.

The F-12 was added to the models and proved a smaller, lighter version of the original tractor built by the company. The various makes quickly established themselves as the F-series and, in 1938, the F-12 was replaced by the F-14, which saw the introduction of an updated steering column and a more powerful engine (with a rev limit of 1,650 rpm).

The F-series lasted until the end of the decade when they were replaced by the Letter-series: A, B, BN, and C and then H, M, and MD. Each model was designed to cope with the workload on various farms, although the tricycle-type front end was retained on the larger models as well as the smaller models, which helped to maintain the machinery's maneuverability. The company even offered a diesel engine (gasoline started the engine and the driver could switch to diesel once the engine was completely warmed up). The Cub was introduced in 1947, the smallest in the line, with a four-cylinder engine and 69-inch wheelbase. The model was designed especially for the company to break into the poor, rural areas in the Deep South, but also proved popular on larger farms where more than one tractor was required. It was an extremely popular model that continued to sell with significant upgrades until the end of the 1970s.

33

■ ABOVE: **A fully restored 1951 International Farmall Cub. The Cub in this form was made from 1947-64 and was a 10 hp light-duty tractor popular with market gardeners. Later models, updated but similar in design, continued to be produced until 1979.**

Fordson

When Henry Ford again turned his attention to tractor production the year was 1915 and the intention was clear: to mass-produce a versatile machine that would dominate the tractor market. The prototype evolved two years later, and due to the Great War, production began in October 1917 for the British Government. The Model F used a 20 hp four-cylinder vaporizing oil engine with a three-speed spur gear transmission, which gave speeds of between 2¼ mph to 6 mph. No brakes were built and drivers were required to stop the vehicle by depressing the clutch. The Model F did not require a heavy separate

■ ABOVE: **Industrial tractors usually ran on solid wheels and tires and were intended for hauling duties in factories. The F was Fordson's first mass-produced tractor and was manufactured from 1917-28.**

frame, which greatly reduced manufacturing costs, although the make was not without its flaws. Like other tractors of the time, the machinery was often not heavy enough to prevent wheel slippage and could rear backwards if the plow met with an obstruction. Some US farmers were so alarmed at the speed that the tractor could flip over that they suggested it was too dangerous for the market and should be banned. The British Government initially ordered 5,000 Fordson Model Fs and around the same time (1917), several issues with the tractor were resolved including enlarging the radiator to reduce overheating problems. Additional weight was added, which

helped to hold the front down while the worm drive – originally located under the driver's seat causing unbearable heat – was relocated, and larger rear wheels became standard in order to improve traction. Fordson models still, however, required a fair amount of maintenance.

Despite the flaws and maintenance, Fordson's Model F is believed by many to be one of the most commercially important designs in tractor history. Perhaps to put this into perspective, the model still dominates conventional tractor design. More than 750,000 Model Fs were sold between 1917 and 1928 – a number still not beaten in tractor sales.

■ ABOVE: A fully restored steel-wheeled 1926 Fordson F tractor.

■ BELOW: A 1925 Fordson F Industrial, a type used widely for road and factory work.

Marshalls

William Marshall, Sons & Company, Lincolnshire, produced its first prototype tractor in 1906 following a long manufacturing history that began in 1848. Designed with an internal combustion engine, the tractor was a two-cylinder gasoline engine, which allowed for plowing one acre an hour (the pulling power of two horses for the same acreage was a day). The company had worldwide recognition for its engineering excellence when it brought its first tractor to market and, by 1910, Marshalls had developed two tractor engines: one was a two-cylinder with 30-35 hp (Class C) and the other was a four-cylinder model with 60-70 hp (Class D). Other models to follow included the two-cylinder (Class E), the Class F that was four cylinders, and the Class G, four-cylinder 70 hp, with two forward gears. Known as the Marshall Colonials, these models were mainly sold to

■ **BELOW: A restored 1876 Marshall 10 hp portable steam engine, effectively the diesel generator of its day.**

Commonwealth countries where concessions saw the company enjoy price advantages over their North American and European competitors. The models were less popular on Britain's domestic market where their heaviness prevented them working well on soft arable soils.

The tractors – of which numbers remain unconfirmed – were mainly sold in North America, Canada, India, Argentina, South Africa, Australia, and Russia where the heavyweights were a success. However, Marshalls' fortunes were to decline, and the Colonials to become outdated, and by 1930 the company was designing and

■ **LEFT:** A line-up of Series 2 Field Marshall tractors from the 1940s. Closest is a 1945 model, then a 1949, and lastly a 1947. Based on the Lanz design, the Field Marshall was a fairly short-lived British design that is now popular with collectors.

■ **BELOW:** At a vintage rally.

manufacturing diesel tractors including the Marshall 15-30 single-cylinder diesel. The tractor did not find success – it was nowhere near as good as its Lanz rival – and the Marshall 18-30 was introduced in 1932 with slight performance improvement in the industry. In 1935, the Marshall 12-20 was brought to market and remained in production until 1938.

Field Marshall tractors were produced between 1945 and 1957 and included the Series 1, Series 2, Series 3, and the Series 3A released in 1952. These Series of tractors found a British market as well as an international audience and were economical to run.

The Moline Universal

The Moline Universal was simply ahead of its time. Produced in Moline, Illinois from 1919, the tractor could boast an electric starter motor, an electric governor, and electric lights. The four-cylinder, 18 hp, with its 1,800 rpm, was truly remarkable with its custom-built electrical system, which housed a 6-volt battery in a battery box that required careful containment. Controls for generator, carburetor, and ignition were located to the right of the engine block, while a master electric switch gear (operating the lights, ignition, and governor) was found in front of the driver. These were all firsts in tractor manufacturing and the average cost of this surprising model

■ OPPOSITE & BELOW: The 1918 Moline Universal D.

■ OPPOSITE BELOW: A 1942 Minneapolis Moline R, a 24 hp row-crop tractor introduced in 1939 that remained in production until at least 1952.

was just a little over $1,320 by 1920 and it is estimated that thousands were sold. A concrete ballast was added inside the drive wheels to lower the vehicle's center of gravity. However, despite its incredible technology for the time, the Moline Universal was never particularly popular and the company suffered during the depression of the early 1920s. Tractor production stopped in 1923 until 1929 when a merger resulted in the Minneapolis-Moline Power Implement Company. The merger proved a success and the company went on to become one the United States' major farm equipment companies until the White Motor Company bought it out in 1963. The Moline Universal D has been popular with restorers and enthusiasts and many are today seen at shows.

Porsche Standard Star

The German Porsche Standard Star with 2,300 rpm was manufactured by Porsche-Diesel-Motorenbau for just three years between 1960 and 1963. The two-cylinder, 30 hp tractor comprised eight forward gears, two reverse gears, and used cutting-edge technology during its day. With its fluid clutch and creeper gears, the Porsche Standard Star was well equipped for maintaining slow steady speeds.

■ ABOVE & BELOW: The Porsche Standard Star 238, 1962.

■ LEFT: The Porsche Standard Star 219.

Steyr 80

Manufactured by Steyr-Daimler-Puch in Austria, the Steyr 80 went into production in 1950. The diesel-powered vehicle was lightweight with a low center of gravity that worked especially well for Alpine farmers. With its four forward gears and one reverse, this one-cylinder tractor had advanced hydraulics and three-point linkage fitted as standard. Weighing in at 2,640 pounds, the Steyr 80 had 15 hp and 1,600 rpm.

■ ABOVE: A vintage Steyr 80.
■ BELOW: A vintage Steyr 15PS, 1955.

■ ABOVE: **A Dutra D4K-A tractor in Hungary.**

■ BELOW: **At work in 1965.**

Dutra

Expansion in the tractor industry was inevitable following the end of World War II and, despite worldwide recovery, sales boomed as more and more farmers switched to mechanized power. Another vital ingredient was post-war prosperity, which further enabled technical improvements. Tractor power became crucial in helping the farming industry recover from the devastation following atrocities, and four-, six-, and eight-wheel

■ **ABOVE:** **A Dutra D4K at a classic meeting in Germany.**

■ **BELOW:** **A Hungarian Dutra D4K.**

drive machines were introduced alongside high-speed diesel engines, high horsepower models, while horse-drawn vehicles were replaced. While this was happening on a grand scale in the USA and the UK, other areas of Europe were also expanding their mechanized capabilities, alongside Russia and East European countries including Hungary, Poland, Czechoslovakia, and Romania.

Based in Hungary, Dutra Tractor Works provided the first 100 hp models seen in Europe, which proved popular in both East and West. The four-wheel drive system employed required large diameter wheels to the front and rear, while the small frame ensured a small steering angle with a big turning circle. East-West collaborations and collectives were not unusual, and Hungary (as well as other East European countries), had a growing demand for large tractors. Based in Budapest, Dutra Tractor Works manufactured tractors between 1961 and 1973. As well as being exported to the UK and other parts of Europe – noticeably France – Dutra models were also exported to New Zealand, and in 1968, through collaboration with Steyr, the DUTRA Steyr model was produced using a Steyr engine.

Utility tractors in engineering and agriculture

■ BELOW: The Bristol 25 crawler tractor was a British-built machine that was in production from 1955 until 1959. This restored example is fitted with a dozer blade.

■ ABOVE: A 1932 Cletrac K tractor fitted with a dozer blade. This is the K20 model but the basic chassis was used for several power options. The K was introduced in 1926 and featured a redesigned track that could be oiled instantaneously for a single plunger oiling point.

Tractors are particularly well suited to engineering work and can be fitted with appropriate tools to enable them to carry out tasks using buckets, hoes, and dozer blades for example. Tractors are referred to as engineering vehicles once they are fitted with these types of tools. Bulldozers, in actual fact, are extremely powerful tractors capable of pushing or dragging large amounts. These engineering vehicles have been developed over a number of years to allow for further heavy-duty work. Loader tractors were fitted with a huge bucket and hydraulic arms to enable the machine to scoop massive quantities of earth and rock for loading into other vehicles. The loader is essentially a tractor with an engineering tool fitted

for large-scale and heavy-duty tasks. The loader was originally adapted from the original bulldozer, and smaller versions have been developed over the years to allow for working environments in limited spaces; others have been further modified to allow for excavation work in small, confined areas.

The hoe loader is another tractor that has seen adaptations to the original in order to better fit the working environment in which it is needed. These vehicles require a loader to the front of the machine and a backhoe to the rear – fixed with a three-point hitch. These industrial-type tractors are extremely heavy vehicles and usually consist of a steel grill and a twisting seat that can be turned around to face the backhoe controls as and when necessary. The main tasks that a backhoe loader might be used for include working in the construction industry, road building and digging, loading other engineering vehicles, paving, demolition, and transportation. Some backhoe buckets have a retractable base, which enables loading to be quicker and more efficient. These timesaving buckets are also often used for grading and scratching sand and can be easily replaced with other implements for different tasks. The backhoe loader is a common engineering vehicle, which is extremely useful in a variety of situations. Its versatility and compact size make it a popular construction tractor. JCB is a

■ BELOW: **This heavy-duty loader with a telescopic arm can lift a 4,000kg load to a height of 7m, making this British-built machine a very versatile piece of construction and farming equipment.**

■ ABOVE: A 1960 John Deere & Hancock 840 scraper used in construction leveling and also in large earth-moving projects in Australia, such as open-cast mines.

■ BELOW: A 1956 Oliver Utility agricultural tractor, a 2004 New Holland TC24D CUT, and a 1993 Cub Cadet.

well-known name in the world of engineering vehicles.

The CUT, or Compact Utility Tractor, is a smaller version of the agricultural tractor and is designed for landscaping and estate management environments. Horsepower of these small, compact tractors is usually between 20 hp and 50 hp with Power Take Off (PTO) horsepower of 15 hp to 45 hp. Compact Utility Tractors are not designed for the use of planting or harvesting on a commercial level and are more commonly used as a finishing mower, a snow blower, or a front-mounted rotary broom. In the United States the tractor has a rear PTO at around 540 rpm, however, in other countries there is an option for around 1,000 rpm

– which is usually standard – however, standard models, in both markets, commonly use a front-end loader. The three-point hitch, with its hydraulic system, is adjustable. CUTs have a four-wheel assist set up, which is basically four-wheel drive and many of the newer versions of this tractor have Hydrostable transmission. These compact tractors also have various models ranging from low-priced

■ **ABOVE:** **A 2006 JCB Robot 190/1110 skid steer loader, a compact and rugged loader for rough or uneven ground conditions. The Robot is also available in wheeled models.**

■ **BELOW:** **A Steyr tractor clearing the roads in Austria.**

■ ABOVE: A modular subsoiler mounted to a New Holland CUT.

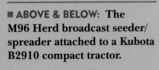

■ ABOVE & BELOW: The M96 Herd broadcast seeder/ spreader attached to a Kubota B2910 compact tractor.

simple gear transmissions to more advanced synchronized transmissions and hi-tech glide shift transmissions. Roll Over Protection Structure (ROPS) comes as standard on modern tractors in just the same way as it would for agricultural vehicles, and in some cases offer the option of a backhoe for specific tasks. In addition, the box blade is quite a common piece of equipment for the Compact Utility Tractor, as is the grader blade, the landscape rake, post hole digger, rotary cutter, finish mower, rotary tiller, sub-soiler, and broadcast seeder. Ideal for large-scale gardening or small-scale farming, some harvesting and planting equipment is specially made for Compact Utility Tractors. In fact, there are an incredible number of implements made for this tractor.

Snow blowers are particularly popular in more northerly climes, but these are usually rear mounted. Powered by a mid-PTO shaft, front-mounted snow blowers are also available. The leading manufacturers of this highly desirable tractor include John Deere, Case, Massey Ferguson, and New Holland Ag.

Row-crop tractors are particularly useful in truck farming where crops are grown for the commercial market in rows. These tractors are essential machinery for cultivating, which can take place soon after the crops have sprouted. During a season, there may be several times that cultivation takes place before the actual rows of crops are harvested. The tractor and the cultivator designed to mount it, are essentially providing a combination of machinery for a specific task, which provides power to make the working environment more efficient. Designed to reduce the hard labor – first carried out by horse-drawn machinery and

■ ABOVE: The John Deere 2520 CUT, with the John Deere 46 backhoe attachment at the rear end and the John Deere 200CX loader at the front end.

■ OPPOSITE ABOVE: A modern John Deere plow. Like all modern plows it has a double row of blades so that it can be rotated when the tractor towing it turns at the end of the furrow, thereby allowing all the furrows to be turned in the same direction.

■ OPPOSITE BELOW: The Fendt Farmer 208V is a compact tractor for small farms, orchards, vineyards, and grounds maintenance. It is powered by an 86 hp engine and is available in various widths; the V indicates a model designed for vineyards. Fendt have had tractors with the Farmer designation in their range for over 50 years.

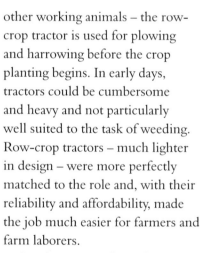

other working animals – the row-crop tractor is used for plowing and harrowing before the crop planting begins. In early days, tractors could be cumbersome and heavy and not particularly well suited to the task of weeding. Row-crop tractors – much lighter in design – were more perfectly matched to the role and, with their reliability and affordability, made the job much easier for farmers and farm laborers.

Another extremely useful utility tractor is the orchard machine designed to travel through fruit and nut orchards, by passing under trees. The tractor is lower to the ground, ensuring that snags from trees are less likely – which is coupled with sheet metal cowlings and fairings that deflect branches – while the exhaust pipes tend to be under-slung.

Mini or garden tractors

■ **ABOVE:** The International Junior was manufactured from 1917 to 1922 and ran on kerosene. Its unusual appearance is largely due to the radiator being mounted behind the motor.

■ **BELOW:** A John Deere LX279 lawn tractor.

Designed for use in domestic gardens, mini tractors, or garden tractors, as they are sometimes known, are primarily used for cutting lawns and come with fitted horizontal rotary cutting decks. The main manufacturers of mini tractors include International Harvester, John Deere, Case, and Massey Ferguson. They look particularly similar to ride-on lawn mowers, however, mini tractors often have a more sturdy design with a stronger frame and axles where transmissions are produced for ground applications rather than just cutting grass. It is possible

to buy a range of equipment for mini tractors including harrows, cultivators, dozer-blades, sweepers, rollers, and rotivators.

These tractors have a one-cylinder or two-cylinder engine (diesel engines are, however, available) and a horizontal crankshaft engine with belt drive. Diesel engines are more widely available throughout Europe while in the United States mid- or rear-engine machines are fairly common and often referred to as "riding lawn mowers." Lawn tractors are, obviously, designed for cutting grass and often house the engine at the front of the machine. Mini tractors usually have multiple mounting bolts on the rear wheels and are capable of using a variety of equipment.

■ ABOVE: A John Deere 4100HST compact tractor.

■ BELOW: A mini tractor, with a snow plow attached, comes to the rescue of Halifax, England.

Two-wheel (single-axle) tractors

Most people envisage tractors with two axles and four wheels, but those with a single axle and two wheels are also technically tractors. It's the power itself – which only requires one axle – that can turn a machine into a tractor. Two-wheel tractors, as these are often known, or single-axle tractors as they can be called, have been in existence since the time of the internal combustion engine. Sometimes also referred to as walk-behind tractors, two-wheel tractors tend to be small, fairly efficient, and affordable. The heyday for two-wheel tractors was primarily prior to the 1960s when they offered a cheaper alternative to two-axle tractors with comparable power. Affordable utility tractors now provide a reasonable alternative, but surprisingly two-wheel tractors still hold a loyal following and they are particularly popular in India, China, and Southeast Asia where they provide a cheap resource, which is easily maintained by the user.

Today, two-wheeled tractors are robust with anti-vibration and adjustable handlebars and a safety lockout system. They are capable of operating a comprehensive range of easy-to-fit equipment for both the front and the rear, and are safe and simple to operate. In addition, new models are proven to work in demanding conditions in an effective and efficient manner.

EPA tractors: Sweden

EPA tractors were developed in Sweden during World War II (1939-1945). These were essentially cars, trucks, and lorries converted and used as a substitute for relatively expensive agricultural machines. Today, the EPA is popular with young people in Sweden who are not yet old enough to drive a car, i.e., for those aged between 15 and 18 years of age. The EPA is a sign of freedom and independence and is very much a part of youth culture. EPAs are also used in the country to tow caravans, which are popular for holidays in the summer months. Simply a vehicle with the passenger space cut away behind the front seats, the EPA tractor was equipped with two gearboxes in a row which, when converted on an older-type vehicle with a ladder frame, was quite similar to a tractor; most essentially, it could be used as one. For the young people of Sweden, it provided a form of transport that from the age of 15 only required a tractor license. Eventually, new EPA tractors were banned, however, those still in existence remained legal vehicles. The A Tractor was introduced into Sweden in 1975 with a top speed of 28 mph.

■ ABOVE: An EPA tractor based on a Volvo Duett.

The modern approach

■ ABOVE: **The rear wheel of a 1918 Ruggles and Parsons tractor. This short-lived model had what the company called "Track Laying Double Traction" wheels that used a system of springs and roller to ensure good traction.**

With new legislation and the introduction of safety cabs, driver safety became an issue during the 1960s, although it would take another 10 to 15 years before comfort and convenience came into play. Today, comfort and safety are priorities for manufacturers, which follow on from the implementation of earlier legislation forced on the tractor industry more than 40 years ago. Developments included cab suspension systems, rubber tracks, turbocharged engines, CVT drive systems, and sprung axles, all of which helped to ensure faster, yet safer working speeds. The early models had no weather protection whatsoever – although some models did attempt a canopy-style roof to protect the driver from rain and, in some cases, the primitive electrical and fuel systems – and the driver and engine remained exposed to the elements. For many decades, the safety and comfort of the driver remained at the bottom of the list of priorities for tractor manufacturers and very few were concerned. Reliability and performance were much more highly regarded by both the companies building the machines and the farmers using them who were reluctant to pay more for a more comfortable seat or a makeshift cab. For those that had toiled all day in the fields with horse-drawn equipment, the arrival of the simple tractor probably seemed improvement enough.

In fact, for more than 50 years, the only improvement to the driver seat on the majority of tractors was a metal seat on a springy steel support. The first tractors to introduce higher-end comfort were Caterpillar – who included padded seats and backrests from the mid 1920s – and Minneapolis-Moline with their "Comfortractor." Progress, however, to universal comfort and safety was slow and it wasn't until Renault Agriculture introduced cabs with full suspension in the 1980s that the industry was once again revolutionized. This Hydrostable cab also enabled faster working speeds and, today,

it is available as standard.

The Silsoe Research Institute (SRI) in Britain were possibly the first to develop the first full suspension system in the tractor's cab, which was designed to alleviate the vibration from the tractor

wheels and so increase faster working speeds and improved comfort for the driver. This cab, despite its success, failed to go into production and Renault Agriculture – who were also developing suspension cabs for

■ BELOW: **A highly-sophisticated modern four-wheel drive tractor with an advanced transmission that allows for up to 32 forward and reverse speeds.**

■ LEFT: A British-built four-wheel drive 135 hp tractor. Typical of the modern farm tractor, it features extreme all-terrain capability and great towing power combined with a comfortable dust-proof, air-conditioned cab.

trucks – visited the British company to exchange ideas. For 10 years the Hydrostable cab was developed by the French and eventually launched in Paris in 1987 at the SIMA Machinery Show. The new system included a combination of coil springs, anti-roll bars, shock absorbers, and transverse rods. Traditionally, farmers suffer from vertical movements from tractor tires, longitudinal movements from towing equipment (such as plowing) at speed, movements linked to large tractors – due to the size of their tires – pitching, and rolling. The Hydrostable cab, it was claimed, could alleviate all such jolting and movements produced by more traditional tractors in the course of the working day.

However, despite proved success, a gold medal from RASE, other awards for innovation, and a generally enthusiastic response to its arrival, sales for the Hydrostable cab remained somewhat slow. It would be 12 years before the cab really found its niche and interest would grow. It seems likely that a number of tests on the Hydrostable cab, carried out in Germany in 1996 by DLG research, acted like a springboard to success. Fastrac tractors, developed by British JCB, soon joined the party with new and important developments in driver comfort. Using Perkins engines, the company's design combined a gearbox with a 45 mph top speed, four-wheel drive through equal wheels, four-wheel braking, and suspension system over both the front and rear axles. This "fast tractor" is designed to meet legal requirements; in many countries, all-round suspension is a legal requirement for safety reasons on fast tractors.

Traditionally, farming in the United States is one of the most dangerous industries in the world and the tractor has had its part to play in hazards facing those involved. With more than 32 percent of farming fatalities caused by tractors – where 50 percent are caused by rollovers and overturns – the dangers are particularly real. ROPS and seat belts are two of the most important safety devices ever introduced to tractors. ROPS stop the operator from being crushed to death in the event of a rollover,

■ BELOW: Here a JCB Fastrac 155-65 tractor is pulling a Case IH LB333 baler making large rectangular bales.

which is especially important in "open" vehicles. Here a steel beam extending over the driver's head is used, while in closed cabs the ROPS is part of the cab and the sides and windows of the cab further protect the operator.

Sweden was the first country to introduce ROPS as legislation in 1959. However, ROPS will only work when the driver stays within the safety framework of the structure. Seat belts are crucial in ensuring that the driver is able to

remain within the framework.

Renault and JCB were beginning to ensure that other manufacturers took notice of suspension systems and their added value, and by the end of the 1990s most, including companies such as John Deere, had

introduced their own systems. John Deere brought in the Triple Link Suspension (TLS) in 1997 with its 6010 Series.

Another crucial development in the tractor industry has to be the use of rubber tracks, which literally initiated a technological revolution for crawlers. Caterpillar made this introduction on the Challenger 65 tractor, which has the gearbox and transmission to the rear axle with large powerful wheels that transmit power to the tracks. The steering mechanism is controlled by a wheel rather than more traditional steering levels and there are three idlers on each side. Production of the Challenger began in 1987 with the Challenger 55, which had a 10-speed transmission and CAT 3306 turbo diesel engine. CLAAS, the German manufacturer, has a special deal with Caterpillar, which sees Challenger marketed throughout Europe in the CLAAS name while combine harvesters are sold in Caterpillar colors in North America.

In Britain, McCormick tractors continue to go from strength to strength. The company was the world's largest tractor exporter throughout much of the 20th century. Moving into the 21st century, McCormick Tractors International began production of the McCormick MC115 in 2001, a four-cylinder turbocharged (complete with Perkins engine) 115 hp model with 16 forward speeds (which rise to 32 with the creeper gear option). But, new manufacturers have joined the tractor revolution alongside

■ **RIGHT: The John Deere 6820 is near the top of the 6020 series and features a high level of driver comfort with cab suspension, noise-reduction, and optional full climate control, a 150 hp turbo diesel motor, and an optional semi-automatic transmission.**

stalwarts like McCormick. These include Multidrive and the Multidrive 6000, first produced in 1999 with its nine-speed gearbox and 155 hp and options for 185 hp, and TYM from Korea in the small- to medium-power sector. Agriculture has also jumped on the space technology bandwagon and GPS devices and on-board computers are now produced as optional extras for farm tractors. They are mainly used in hi-tech precision farming techniques, including in automation in plowing, and for the use of auto-steering systems which are required at the ends of rows to prevent overlapping and using more fuel than necessary and to avoid leaving streaks when cultivating.

The future for the tractor industry is incredibly hard to predict. All kinds of developments are likely. Many have tried over the years to foresee the future for the industry; some have been right in their predictions while others have been widely wrong in their assumptions. Some things are clear however, there will be more and more demand for larger and more powerful tractors designed for vast farms, especially in North America, and classic tractors will remain forever in the hearts of those who love them and the history of agriculture, and the machines that made it possible will be preserved for many generations to come.

■ ABOVE: A 2004 John Deere 7920. A state-of-the-art modern tractor with an enormous range of options and great pulling power.

Useful websites

Classic Tractor Fever
http://www.classictractors.com/

Wilke's Classic Tractors
http://wilkesclassictractors.com

The Ferguson Club
http://www.fergusonclub.com/

Yesterday's Tractors
http://www.ytmag.com/

The Society of Ploughmen
http://www.ploughmen.co.uk/

Ford and Fordson Ireland
http://www.fordfordsonireland.com/

Friends of Ferguson Heritage
http://www.fofh.co.uk/

Zetor Club UK
http://www.zetorclub.co.uk/

DMR Machinery Club (DB/Case/IH)
http://www.dmr-tractor-club.co.uk/

The National Vintage Tractor & Engine Club
http://www.nvtec.co.uk/

Antique Tractors Online
http://antiquetractorsonline.com/

World Ploughing Organisation
http://www.worldploughing.org/

Vintage Horticultural Garden Machinery Club
http://www.vhgmc.co.uk/